Mina's Day

by Kim Borland

PEARSON

Scott
Foresman

Editorial Offices: Glenview, Illinois • Parsippany, New Jersey • New York, New York
Sales Offices: Needham, Massachusetts • Duluth, Georgia • Glenview, Illinois
Coppell, Texas • Ontario, California • Mesa, Arizona

Every effort has been made to secure permission and provide appropriate credit for photographic material. The publisher deeply regrets any omission and pledges to correct errors called to its attention in subsequent editions.

Unless otherwise acknowledged, all photographs are the property of Scott Foresman, a division of Pearson Education.

Photo locators denoted as follows: Top (T), Center (C), Bottom (B), Left (L), Right (R), Background (Bkgd)

Opener (TL) ©Charles & Josette Lenars/Corbis; Opener (BR) ©Paul Hurd/Stone/Getty Images; 1 ©Michael S. Yamashita/Corbis; 3 ©Charles & Josette Lenars/Corbis; 4 ©Jose Fuste Raga/Corbis; 6 Getty Images; 7 ©Paul Hurd/Stone/Getty Images; 8 ©Michael S. Yamashita/Corbis; 9 ©Bohemian Nomad Picturemakers/Corbis; 10 ©Michael S. Yamashita/Corbis; 11 ©Chung Sung-Jun/Getty Images; 12 ©Ronnie Kaufman/Corbis

ISBN: 0-328-13266-7

5 6 7 8 9 10 V010 14 13 12 11 10 09 08 07

Hello! My name is Mina. I am seven years old.

I live in South Korea. My home is in a large city called Seoul.

Korea is made up of two countries: North Korea and South Korea.

I like living in Seoul. Some things here are old and some things are new. In Seoul, there are tall, shiny, new buildings. There are also buildings from long ago.

The summers are very hot. The winters are long and cold. We call June, July, and August the rainy season. Why? The answer is that sometimes it rains almost every day for a month!

I live with my parents, my two brothers, and my baby sister.

My family and I like to play games together. Our favorite game is *yut*. You throw sticks into the air.

Your score depends on which way your sticks land.

In the game of *yut*, each stick has a smooth side and a rough side.

My friends and I often walk to school together. We keep one another company on the long walk.

At the morning meeting, the principal shares important news with everyone. Then children bow, thank the principal, and go off to class.

When we get to school, we go to the playground. There we have a morning meeting.

After school, students stay and help clean. We empty trash cans, sweep the floors, and wash the blackboards.

Korean children go to school on Saturday morning too.

I would love to show you the Palace of Shining Happiness. I think it is the most beautiful place anywhere! People visit all the time to learn about the kings and queens of long ago.

The palace was once the home of the royal family.

On weekends, the palace is filled with people. Many come from faraway places.

Many visitors want to take a picture before they go.

Long ago, the Palace of Shining Happiness was made up of 500 buildings!

One of the most important holidays in Korea is New Year's Day.

We visit with friends and family. We make kites together.

Making and flying kites are traditional parts of the Korean New Year's celebration.

Kite flying is my favorite part of the celebration. We all make wishes for the new year as the kites float high into the air.

Traditional Korean kites are shaped like rectangles. Many have colorful drawings.